DISCOVER
MERMAIDS
DO YOU BELIEVE?

This series features creatures that excite our minds. They're magic. They're myth. They're mystery. They're also not real. They live in our stories.

45TH PARALLEL PRESS

Published in the United States of America by Cherry Lake Publishing Group
Ann Arbor, Michigan
www.cherrylakepublishing.com

Reading Adviser: Beth Walker Gambro, MS Ed., Reading Consultant, Yorkville, IL
Book Design: Felicia Macheske

Photo Credits: © Willyam Bradberry,Shutterstock.com, cover, 8; © tsuneomp/Shutterstock.com, cover; © schankz/ Shutterstock, 1; © Olga Nikonova/Shutterstock, 1; © Alex Pix/Shutterstock, 5; © Gehrke/Shutterstock, 6; © Michael Bogner/Shutterstock, 6; © Melkor3D/Shutterstock, 11; © Jaroslaw Grudzinski/Shutterstock, 13; © Dmitry Laudin/ Shutterstock, 15; © Sergii Figurnyi/Shutterstock, 17; © Rudchenko Liliia/Shutterstock, 18; © prapann/Shutterstock, 20

Graphic Elements Throughout: © denniro/Shutterstock; © Libellule/Shutterstock; © sociologas/Shutterstock; © paprika/Shutterstock; © ilolab/Shutterstock; © Bruce Rolff/Shutterstock

45th Parallel Press is an imprint of Cherry Lake Publishing.

Library of Congress Cataloging-in-Publication Data

Names: Loh-Hagan, Virginia, author.
Title: Discover mermaids / Virginia Loh-Hagan.
Description: Ann Arbor, Michigan : Cherry Lake Publishing, [2023] | Series: Magic, myth, and mystery express | Audience: Grades 2-3 | Summary: "How does a mermaid kiss help a drowning sailor? Why do mermaids usually carry a mirror? Books in the Magic, Myth, and Mystery Express series for young readers explore spooky creatures that go bump in the night, fill our dreams (or nightmares!), and make us afraid of the dark. Written with a high-interest level to appeal to a more mature audience and a lower level of complexity, clear visuals help struggling readers along. Considerate text includes fascinating information and wild facts to hold readers' interest and support comprehension. Includes table of contents, glossary with simplified pronunciations, and index"— Provided by publisher.
Identifiers: LCCN 2022039538 | ISBN 9781668919644 (hardcover) | ISBN 9781668920664 (paperback) | ISBN 9781668921999 (ebook) | ISBN 9781668923320 (pdf)
Subjects: LCSH: Mermaids—Juvenile literature. | Animals, Mythical—Juvenile literature.
Classification: LCC GR910 .L64 2023 | DDC 398.21—dc23/eng/20220826
LC record available at https://lccn.loc.gov/2022039538

Cherry Lake Publishing would like to acknowledge the work of the Partnership for 21st Century Learning, a network of Battelle for Kids. Please visit *http://www.battelleforkids.org/networks/p21* for more information.

Printed in the United States of America
Corporate Graphics

Dr. Virginia Loh-Hagan is an author, university professor, former classroom teacher, and curriculum designer. Her favorite fairy tale is *The Little Mermaid*. She lives in San Diego with her very tall husband and very naughty dogs.

CONTENTS

CHAPTER ONE
Under the Sea..................... **4**

CHAPTER TWO
**More than
Swimming Beauties** **10**

CHAPTER THREE
Managing Mermaids **14**

CHAPTER FOUR
Fishy Tales............................ **18**

Consider This! **23**

Learn More... **23**

Glossary.. **23**

Index **24**

Under the Sea

Mermaids are magic sea creatures. They have a woman's head and upper body. They have a fish tail. They live in oceans and seas. They live in rivers and lakes.

Mermaid *comes from an Old English word.* Mere *means sea.* Maid *means a young woman.*

Mermaids are beautiful. They're young. They carry mirrors. They like to look in the mirrors.

Some have webbed hands. They have large, forked tails. Their whole bodies **shimmer**. Shimmer means to shine.

Mermaids adapt to the waters they live in.

Explained by
SCIENCE

Humans can't breathe underwater. Fish can. Fish use gills to breathe. The gills remove the oxygen for the fish to use.

There are different types of mermaids. Most mermaids only live in the sea. Some mermaids are **shapeshifters**. They can change into humans at any time. They can live in water and on land.

Some mermaids have more dolphin-like tails.

Did You KNOW?

Blackbeard was a famous pirate. Some people think he ordered his ships to avoid mermaids.

CHAPTER TWO

More than Swimming Beauties

Mermaids guide ships. Mermaids have saved drowning sailors. They kiss the sailors. This allows sailors to breathe underwater. They also do bad things. They cause shipwrecks.

Some sailors thought mermaids were bad omens.

Have You
HEARD?

Explorers thought they saw mermaids. But they really saw **manatees**. These ocean animals have tails like paddles. They have flippers that look like stubby arms.

Mermaids are smart. They use tools. They make weapons from things found in the sea. They make **tridents**. Tridents are spears with 3 points.

Full moons can grant mermaids extra or stronger powers.

CHAPTER THREE

Managing Mermaids

Mermaids lose power on land. They get confused. They can't be in the sun all day. They get weak. They die. So they stay near water. Water makes them strong.

Mermaids have strong night vision. They can see in the total darkness of the deep sea.

Mermaids love being in love. Male mermaids are called **mermen**. There aren't many mermen. So mermaids fall in love with humans.

STAY SAFE!

- Give mermaids sparkly gifts. This will keep them busy.

- Get a mermaid to fall in love with a human male. They'll be distracted by love.

Mermaids go on land to look for love. This makes them weak. Some mermaids have lost their lives for love.

A mermaid's weakest spot is the center of her head.

Fishy Tales

Hans Christian Andersen wrote fairy tales. He wrote *The Little Mermaid*. This is a famous mermaid story. Andersen's mermaid saved a drowning prince. She fell in love with him.

Pictures of Atargatis show her as a fishy human.

ORIGINS

The first mermaid was Atargatis. Her story came from ancient Syria. Atargatis was a goddess. She wanted to become a fish. The gods wouldn't let her give up her beauty. So only her bottom half became a fish.

She went to a sea witch. She asked the witch for legs. She traded her voice for them. But the prince chose another woman. The mermaid died from a broken heart. She became sea foam.

There are many different ideas about how mermaids came to be.

Know the LINGO!

Kelpie: a water spirit in Scottish folk stories that looks like a horse and drowns people

Merfolk: mermaids and mermen

Merrow: the Irish and English name for merfolk

Real
WORLD

Weeki Wachee Springs is in South Florida. Professional mermaids work here. Their job is to pretend to be mermaids!

CONSIDER THIS!

Say What?

Explain how mermaids are like fish. Explain how they're like humans. Do you think they're more humans or fish? Explain your reasoning.

Think About It!

In some stories, mermaids are peaceful and beautiful. In other stories, mermaids are evil. Do you think they're more good or more evil?

LEARN MORE

Claybourne, Anna, and Miren Asiain Lora. *The Mermaid Atlas: Merfolk of the World*. London: Laurence King Publishing Ltd, 2020.

Hawkins, Emily. *A Natural History of Mermaids*. London: Frances Lincoln, 2022.

Laskow, Sarah, and Reimena Yee. *The Very Short, Entirely True History of Mermaids*. New York: Penguin Workshop, 2020.

Glossary

manatees (MA-nuh-teez) underwater mammals with a rounded tail flipper

mermen (MUHR-mehn) male versions of mermaids

shapeshifters (SHAYP-shif-tuhrs) creatures that can change their shapes

shimmer (SHIH-muhr) to shine or glitter

tridents (TRY-duhnts) three-pronged spears

Index

Andersen, Hans Christian, 18, 20
Atargatis, 18, 19

Blackbeard, 9
breathing, 7, 10

fish, 7, 18–19

gills, 7

humans, 7, 8, 15, 16, 18, 20, 22

kelpies, 21

Little Mermaid, The (tale), 18, 20
love, 15, 16, 17, 18, 20

manatees, 12
mermen and merfolk, 15, 21

merrow, 21

pirates, 9

sailors, 10
shapeshifters, 8, 21
ships, 10–11

tails, 4, 5, 6, 8, 12, 19
tales, 18–20
traits and powers, 4, 6, 8, 13, 14, 16, 17
tridents, 13

waters, 4, 6, 14
Weeki Wachee Springs, 22